JUMPIN' JIM'S UKULELE SPIRIT

Compiled and Arranged by Jim Beloff

 sing unto the Lord a new song,
For he hath done marvelous things.

— *Psalm Ninety-Eight*

HAL•LEONARD®
CORPORATION
7777 W. BLUEMOUND RD. P.O. BOX 13819 MILWAUKEE, WI 53213

Edited by Ronny S. Schiff
Cover and Art Direction by Elizabeth Maihock Beloff
Graphics and Music Typography by Charylu Roberts

Foreword

The first song I teach at a ukulele workshop is usually "He's Got The Whole World In His Hands." There are a few reasons for this. The first is that it is a two-chord song, which makes it one of the easiest songs to learn to play on the ukulele—and virtually everyone knows the melody and words. Also, on a personal level, I like to think that playing the uke is a little like having the whole world in your hands. Anyway, the combination of message, familiarity, ease of play and simple beauty have made "He's Got The Whole World" a favorite song.

Interestingly enough, when we began to look at other famous songs that come from the gospel and spiritual traditions, it turned out that many of them shared similar qualities. Most importantly, these beautiful songs seemed just as heartfelt when strummed on a humble ukulele. At the same time we also began to hear more and more from folks who were playing gospel music on their ukes, even in church. Then September 11th, 2001 happened. Soon after, the idea of people singing and playing music together (like they used to in the days when community songbooks were plentiful) seemed more appropriate than ever. Suddenly, songs about peace and faith took on a greater resonance.

One of the best parts about publishing these songbooks is getting to learn and live with whole new categories of songs. Sometimes, though, it is the songs we've always known that, under fresh scrutiny, truly amaze. There is a reason, for example, that we all know "This Little Light Of Mine." That's because it is, very simply, a great song—great message, unforgettable melody and a real pleasure to play on the ukulele. Here's to your raising many spirits singing and strumming these songs. *Peace, Shalom, Shanti, Salaam!*

This songbook has been nurtured by a number of great spirits. First and foremost, a big thank you to Pat Boone for your willingness to share your ukulele story with us. Also to my wife, Liz Beloff, who imagined and saw the need for this songbook. Many folks helped with song suggestions including Stephen and Sandy Arterburn, Mimi Kennedy, Larry Dilg, Tracy and Monty Maples, Audrey and Don Maihock, John Zehnder, Larry D., Darrell Grob, CeCe Critchley Oler and especially Kim Oler whose two magnificent songs we are particularly happy to present here. As always, thanks to Charylu Roberts, Wendy DeWitt, and Ronny Schiff.

—Jumpin' Jim Beloff
Los Angeles, CA 2002

Also Available: (Books) *Jumpin' Jim's Ukulele Favorites; Jumpin' Jim's Ukulele Tips 'n' Tunes; Jumpin' Jim's Ukulele Gems; Jumpin' Jim's Ukulele Christmas; Jumpin' Jim's '60s Uke-In; Jumpin' Jim's Gone Hawaiian; Jumpin' Jim's Camp Ukulele; Jumpin' Jim's Ukulele Masters: Lyle Ritz; Jumpin' Jim's Ukulele Beach Party; Jumpin' Jim's Ukulele Masters: Herb Ohta; Jumpin' Jim's Ukulele Masters: Lyle Ritz Solos; The Ukulele: A Visual History.* **(CDs)** *Jim's Dog Has Fleas; For The Love Of Uke; Legends Of Ukulele; It's A Fluke; Lyle Ritz & Herb Ohta—A Night Of Ukulele Jazz.* **(Video)** *The Joy Of Uke.*

For all inquiries: Flea Market Music, Inc., Box 1127, Studio City, CA. 91614.
Visit us on the web at www.fleamarketmusic.com

Pat Boone On Ukuleles

My love affair with the ukulele even pre-dates the one I've had with my wife for fifty years — and that's quite a love story!

My mama taught me the few chords she had learned from comic actress Judy Canova when she was a little girl, and my brother Nick and I took turns fanning those few chords and trying to invent others from the time we were 8 or 10 years old, respectively. Though we only knew a few basic chords, we could strum pretty impressively, and we would entertain at family gatherings and sometimes casual school functions, while we were growing up. I think there's no doubt that those experiences set the stage for my entertainment career, helping me to get past the normal reticence and nerves most kids would feel performing in front of various groups.

On our senior trip to Washington D.C., I kept our whole bus load of David Lipscomb High seniors singing from Nashville to D.C., and it was an absolute blast! After we checked into the hotel, and seeing that the nation's capital was absolutely teeming with other high school seniors from all over the country in a very boisterous mood, I looked around the snug little fourth-story hotel room for a safe place to hide my baritone Martin. I was sharing that little room with another guy, and most of the doors were open up and down the hall, so I cannily stashed my "orchestra" deep under the bed, against the wall. I was sure it was safe and secure, ready for whatever happened with other kids in Washington— and then, of course, for our long bus ride home.

What happened next still causes me to wince (and get angry as well).

Bayron Binkley, nice enough guy, but the loudest and most irrepressible (I'm trying to be kind) fella in our class, came charging down the hall, arms flailing and yelling at the top of his voice, entered our door and took a flying leap into the middle of our bed. You guessed it— the bed collapsed right on top of my ukulele, and crushed it into splinters!

I was stunned speechless, and though Bayron apologized profusely, the damage was done and my "little brother" was dead. I can tell you, that was one long sad ride back to Nashville.

I've had a number of ukuleles since then, and have one now in Hawaii and here in L.A., but somehow I've never found another that matched the sweet tone and warmth and "fit" of that first beautiful uke.

But the love affair continues…

Pat Boone

1/28/02

Biography

Pat Boone has been sharing his faith through music for most of his life. At 14 he became the song leader at his hometown Nashville, Tennessee Church of Christ and continued there even as his own pop music career was taking off. Eventually that pop career would lead him to sell more records in the 1950s than any other artist except Elvis Presley.

He made hits of songs as diverse as "Ain't That A Shame," "Tutti Frutti" and "Love Letters In The Sand." His multi-faceted career included starring roles in films such as *April Love, Journey To The Center Of The Earth* and *Bernardine* where he even strummed a ukulele. Along the way, he appeared for a year and a half on the Arthur Godfrey show and eventually was awarded his own ABC weekly musical variety show. He has written best-selling books and penned the lyrics to the classic movie theme song, "Exodus."

Through it all, though, Pat Boone has maintained a devout love of gospel songs and spirituals. Recorded early in his career, his *Hymns We Love* album is one of the best-selling gospel records of all time.

Currently Pat oversees a very successful record company, The Gold Label, and continues to host radio and television gospel music shows. A famously devoted husband and father, his name has also become synonymous with a variety of charitable causes. To this day, his message is one of music, compassion, love and faith.

Mama taught me my first few chords, and I've always felt I sang best to the mellow sound of the ukulele.
—*Pat Boone*

Sunday School

In the beginning...

The songs in this book are arranged for ukuleles in C tuning. In this tuning, the individual strings from top (closest to your head) to bottom (closest to your feet) are tuned GCEA. One of the best things about the ukulele is that it is so easy to play. A lot of chords can be made with one or two fingers and many of the songs in this book can be played with three or four chords.

C or 3rd → E or 2nd
G or 4th → A or 1st
Nut
Frets
Position Dots
Neck
Pick or strum within this area
Sound Hole
Names of Strings
A
E
C
G
Bridge
4th 3rd 2nd 1st

Uke C Tuning:

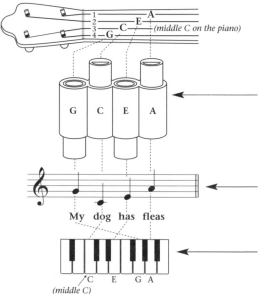

1 — A
2 — E
3 — C
4 — G
(middle C on the piano)

G C E A

My dog has fleas

C E G A
(middle C)

The easiest way to tune the ukulele is with a pitchpipe, matching the strings with the notes.

This corresponds to that famous melody...

Here are the notes on the keyboard.

To get the best sound out of your ukulele, make sure you are in tune. As soon as you are in tune, try holding the ukulele like the person below.

For best results, the neck of your ukulele should be aimed at approximately 2:00. Press your uke against you with the middle of your forearm. Your strumming hand should fall naturally on top of the highest frets, not directly over the soundhole as first timers often think. Hold the neck of the uke between your thumb and first finger of your other hand so that your other fingers are free to move about the fretboard.

1 = Index finger
2 = Second finger
3 = Ring finger
4 = Pinky
0 = Open string (no fingers)

You make chords by putting different combinations of fingers on the fretboard. In this book, you'll find chord diagrams that show you where to put your fingers to get the right sound. The vertical lines in the diagrams represent strings and the horizontal lines represent frets. The numbers at the bottom of the chords shown below indicate what fingers to use.

C Chord

0 0 0 3

F Chord

2 0 1 0

G7 Chord

0 2 1 3

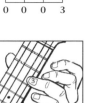

Golden Rules

1. When pressing down the strings, use the tips of the fingers.
2. Always press down in the space between the frets, not on them.
3. Press the strings down to the fingerboard.
4. If you hear a buzz, you may not be pressing down hard enough, or you may be too close to the fret.
5. Keep the thumb at the back of the neck, parallel to the frets.

Playing the ukulele requires two simultaneous actions: One is forming the chords. The second is strumming the strings. Most of the songs in this book can be strummed with the "common strum." This is basically a down-up motion with the pad of the thumb strumming downward on the strings, and then the pad of the index finger coming up on them. (For more strumming techniques, refer to *Jumpin' Jim's Ukulele Tips 'n' Tunes*.)

Chord Choir

Tune Ukulele
G   C   E   A

MAJOR CHORDS

A A#/Bb B C C#/Db D D#/Eb E F F#/Gb G G#/Ab

MINOR CHORDS

Am A#m/Bbm Bm Cm C#m/Dbm Dm D#m/Ebm Em Fm F#m/Gbm Gm G#m/Abm

DOMINANT SEVENTH CHORDS

A7 A#7/Bb7 B7 C7 C#7/Db7 D7 D#7/Eb7 E7 F7 F#7/Gb7 G7 G#7/Ab7

DOMINANT NINTH CHORDS

A9 A#9/Bb9 B9 C9 C#9/Db9 D9 D#9/Eb9 E9 F9 F#9/Gb9 G9 G#9/Ab9

MINOR SEVENTH CHORDS

Am7 A#m7/Bbm7 Bm7 Cm7 C#m7/Dbm7 Dm7 D#m7/Ebm7 Em7 Fm7 F#m7/Gbm7 Gm7 G#m7/Abm7

MAJOR SIXTH CHORDS

A6 A#6/Bb6 B6 C6 C#6/Db6 D6 D#6/Eb6 E6 F6 F#6/Gb6 G6 G#6/Ab6

MINOR SIXTH CHORDS

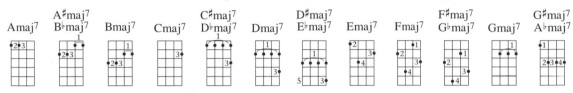

MAJOR SEVENTH CHORDS

DOMINANT SEVENTH CHORDS WITH RAISED FIFTH (7th+5)

DOMINANT SEVENTH CHORDS WITH LOWERED FIFTH (7th-5)

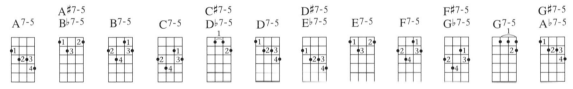

AUGMENTED FIFTH CHORDS (aug or +)

DIMINISHED SEVENTH CHORDS (dim)

All You Need Is Love

Words and Music by
JOHN LENNON and PAUL McCARTNEY

Love, love, love, love, love, love. Love, love, love, love, love, love, love.

There's noth-ing you can do that can't be done,
There's noth-ing you can know that is - n't known,

noth-ing you can sing that can't be sung.
noth-ing you can see that is - n't shown.

Noth-ing you can say but you can learn how to
No - where you can be that is - n't where _____ you're

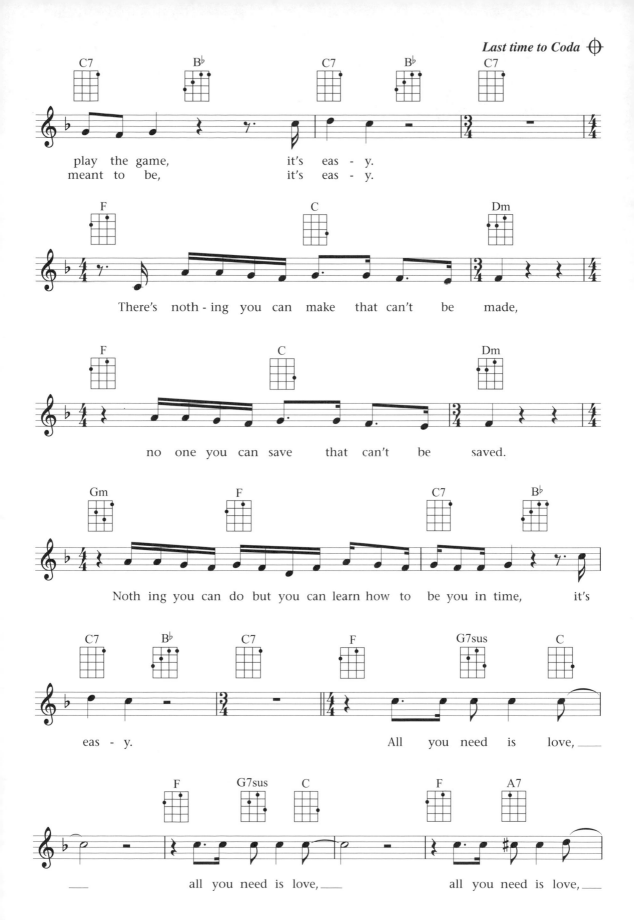

play the game,   *it's eas - y.*
meant to be,   *it's eas - y.*

There's noth - ing you can make that can't be made,

no one you can save that can't be saved.

Noth ing you can do but you can learn how to be you in time,   *it's*

eas - y.   *All you need is love, ___*

___ all you need is love, ___   *all you need is love, ___*

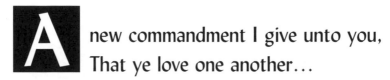

A new commandment I give unto you,
That ye love one another...
– John 13:34

Amazing Grace

Words by
JOHN NEWTON

Traditional
American Melody

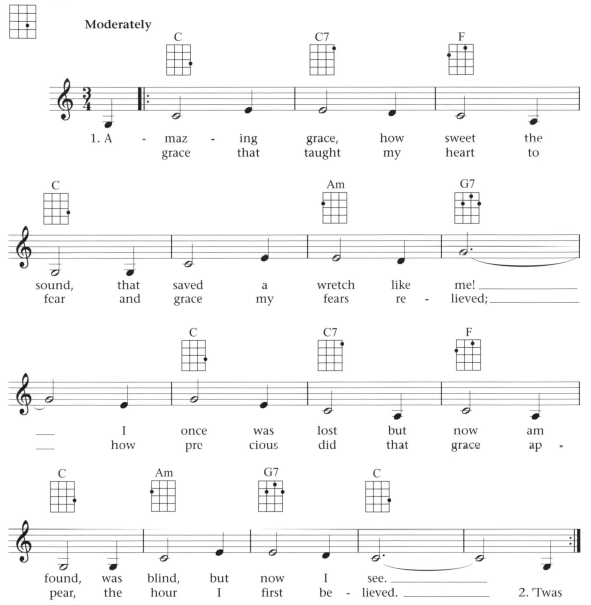

Additional Lyrics

3. Through many dangers, toils, and snares
   I have already come;
   'twas grace that brought me safe thus far,
   and grace will lead me home.

4. When we've been there ten thousand years,
   bright shining as the sun,
   we've no less days to sing God's praise,
   than when we first begun.

Amen

Words and Music by
JESTER HAIRSTON

See Him in the tem - ple, talk - in' with the el - ders,
men. A - men,

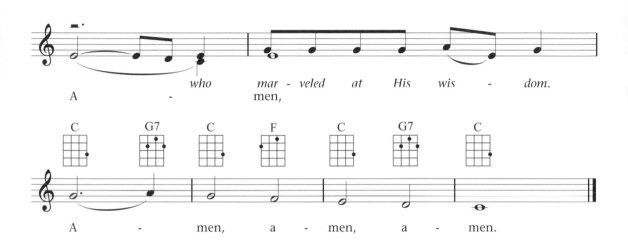

who mar - veled at His wis - dom.
A - men,

A - men, a - men, a - men.

Additional Lyrics

2. See Him at the Jordan,
   where John was baptizin'
   and savin' all the sinners.
   See Him at the seaside,
   talkin' with the fishermen
   and makin' them disciples.

3. Marchin' in Jerusalem
   over palm branches
   in pomp and splendor.
   See Him in the garden,
   prayin' to His Father
   in deepest sorrow.

4. Led before Pilate,
   then they crucified Him,
   but He rose on Easter.
   Hallelujah,
   He died to save us,
   and He lives forever.

Balm In Gilead

Traditional

Blue Green Hills Of Earth

The text was inspired by astronaut Rusty Schweickert, who quoted Heinlein's mythical poet, Rhysling, describing the "cool green hills of Earth" on a return from orbit.

Words and Music by
KIM OLER

FIRST NOTE

With a Gospel Feel

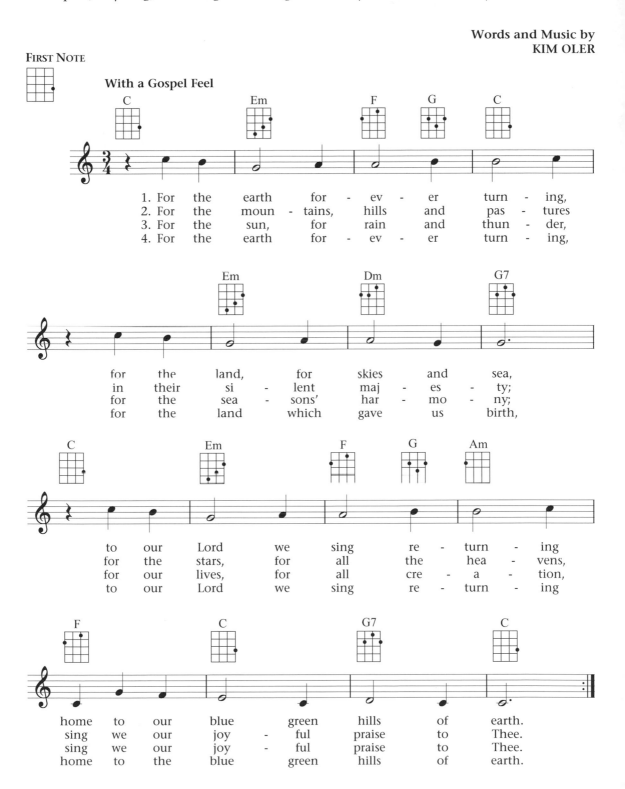

1. For the earth for - ev - er turn - ing,
2. For the moun - tains, hills and pas - tures
3. For the sun, for rain and thun - der,
4. For the earth for - ev - er turn - ing,

for the land, for skies and sea,
in their si - lent maj - es - ty;
for the sea - sons' har - mo - ny;
for the land which gave us birth,

to our Lord we sing re - turn - ing
for the stars, for all the hea - vens,
for our lives, for all cre - a - tion,
to our Lord we sing re - turn - ing

home to our blue green hills of earth.
sing we our joy - ful praise to Thee.
sing we our joy - ful praise to Thee.
home to the blue green hills of earth.

Closer To The Light

Words by
JIM BELOFF

Music by
HERB OHTA

Moderately, with feeling

Oh, from day to day, it's so hard for me to say, ___
Ev - 'ry day I start, with this com - pass in my heart, ___

___ if the road that I'm on now ___ will lead me right. ___
___ and it helps me keep the road ___ with - in my sight. ___

Oh, but year to year, it be -
And as I go forth look - ing

comes a bit more clear, ___ looks like I am get - ting clos -
for mag - ne - tic north, ___ I feel I am get - ting clos -

er   to   the   light.

er   to   the   light.   And   when   my

bur - den's   great,   so   that   I   bend____   un - der   the   weight,____

____   and   it   seems   like   I'm   sur - round - ed   by   the   night.____

_____   Oh   well,   I   don't   mind   trav - el - ing   a - long____

____   this   dark - ened   road,_____   if   I'm   trav' - ling

D.C. al Fine

Fine

clos - er   to   the   light._____

Day By Day

Words and Music by
STEPHEN SCHWARTZ

day by day,_____ oh, dear Lord three

things I pray:_____ to see Thee more

clear - ly,_____ love Thee more dear - ly,_____

fol - low Thee more near - ly,_____

day by day._____ Day by day_____ by

day by day_____ by day._____

Down By The Riverside

Traditional

First Note

With Feeling

1. Gon - na lay down my sword and shield____ down by the riv - er - side,____ down by the riv - er - side,____ down by the riv - er - side.____ Gon - na lay down my sword and shield____ down by the riv - er - side,____ and stud-y____ war no more.____

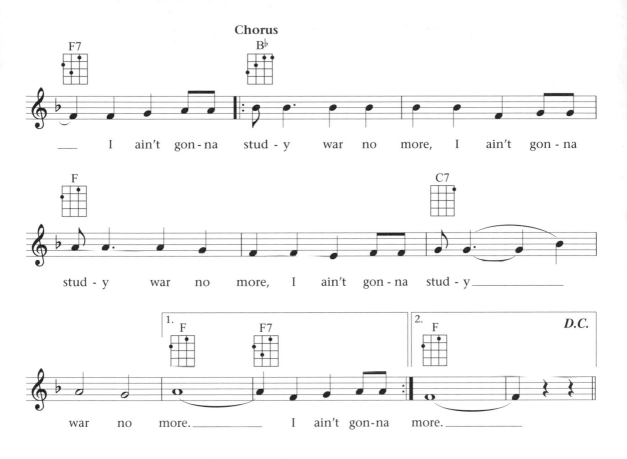

Chorus

I ain't gon-na stud-y war no more, I ain't gon-na stud-y war no more, I ain't gon-na stud-y

1. war no more. I ain't gon-na more.

2. war no more.

Additional Lyrics

2. I'm gonna join hands with everyone,
   down by the riverside, down by the riverside,
   down by the riverside.
   I'm gonna join hands with everyone,
   down by the riverside,
   and study war no more.

And they shall beat their swords into plowshares, and their spears into pruninghooks: nation shall not lift up sword against nation, neither shall they learn war any more.

—Isaiah: 2:4

Ev'ry Time I Feel The Spirit

Traditional

Ev - 'ry time I_____ feel the spir - it,_____ mov - in'

in my heart,_____ I will pray._____ Ev - 'ry

time I_____ feel the spir - it,_____ mov - in' in my heart,_____ I will

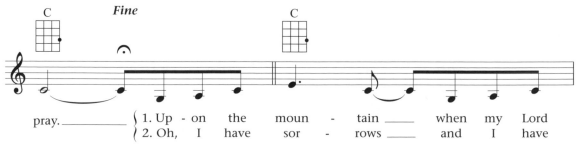

pray._____ 1. Up - on the moun - tain _____ when my Lord
2. Oh, I have sor - rows _____ and I have

G7

spoke,_____ out of His mouth came_____ fire and
woe,_____ and I have heart - ache_____ here be -

C

smoke._____ Looked all a - round me,____ it looked so
low;_____ but while God leads me,____ I'll nev - er

Last time
D.S. al Fine

G7   C

fine,____ 'til I asked my Lord____ if all were mine.____ Ev - 'ry
fear,_____ for I am shel - tered____ by___ His care.____

Dona Nobis Pacem
(Grant Us Peace)

Old German Canon

Slowly
(May be sung as a three-part round)

Do - na no - bis pa - cem, pa - cem,

do - na___ no - bis pa - cem.

Do - na no - bis pa - cem, do - na no - bis

pa - cem. Do - na no - bis___

pa - cem; do - na no - bis pa - cem.

He's Got The Whole World
In His Hands

Traditional

FIRST NOTE

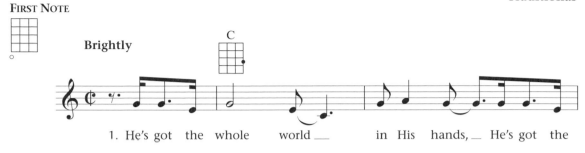

1. He's got the whole world __ in His hands, __ He's got the whole world __ in His hands, __ He's got the whole world __

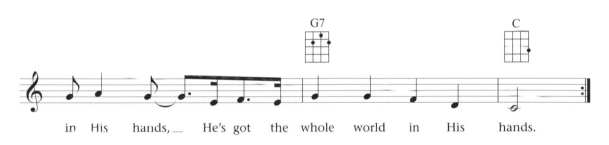

in His hands, __ He's got the whole world in His hands.

Additional Lyrics

2. He's got the little bitty baby in His hands…

3. He's got you and me, sister, in His hands…

4. He's got you and me, brother, in His hands…

5. He's got a little ukulele in His hands…

6. He's got the whole world in His hands…

Hevenu Shalom Aleichem

"Shalom" in Hebrew can be translated as "Hello,"
"Goodbye" or "Peace." In this song the words mean "Peace unto you."

D7   Gm

He - ve - nu sha - lom a - lei - chem, _____

A7

he - ve - nu sha - lom a -

Dm   A7

lei - chem, _____ he - ve - nu sha - lom,

Dm

sha - lom, sha - lom a - lei - chem!

Jerusalem, Old City

29

How Great Thou Art

Words and Music by
STUART K. HINE

1. Oh Lord my God! When I in awe-some
2. When through the woods and for-est glades I
3. And when I think that God, His Son not
4. When Christ shall come with shout of ac-cla-

won-der_____ con-sid-er all the worlds Thy hands have
wan-der_____ and hear the birds sing sweet-ly in the
spar-ing,_____ sent Him to die, I scarce can take it
ma-tion_____ and take me home, what joy shall fill my

made;_____ I see the stars, I hear the roll-ing
trees;_____ when I look down from loft-y moun-tain
in;_____ that on the cross my bur-den glad-ly
heart!_____ Then I shall bow in hum-ble ad-o-

thun-der,_____ Thy pow'r through-out the u-ni-verse dis-
gran-deur_____ and hear the brook and feel the gen-tle
bear-ing,_____ He bled and died to take a-way my
ra-tion_____ and there pro-claim my God how great Thou

played... ⎫
breeze... ⎪
sin... ⎬ Then sings my soul, my Sav - ior God to
art! ⎭

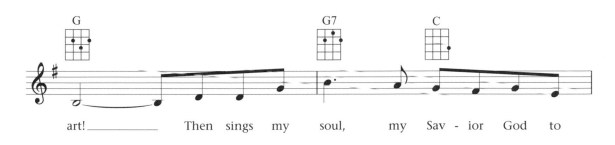

Thee,_____ how great Thou art,_____ how great Thou

art!_____ Then sings my soul, my Sav - ior God to

Thee,_____ how great Thou art,_____ how great Thou art._____

Hinei Ma Tov

Traditional
Psalm 133

1. Hi - nei ma tov u - ma na - im,
2. How good it is and how pleas - ant when

she - vet a - chim gam ya - chad.
peo - ple can live to - geth - er.

Hi - nei ma tov,
How good it is when

she - vet a - chim gam ya - chad.
peo - ple can live to - geth - er.

I'll Fly Away

Words and Music by
ALBERT E. BRUMLEY

1. Some glad morn-ing when this life is o'er,_____
2. Just a few more wea-ry days and then,_____

I'll fly a-way. To a home on God's ce-les-tial shore,
I'll fly a-way. To a land where joy shall nev-er end,

I'll fly a-way.
I'll fly a-way. } I'll fly a-way, o glo-ry,

I'll fly a-way. When I die, hal-le-lu-jah by and by, oh,___

1.
I'll fly a-way.

2.
way.

*optional

I Believe

Words and Music by
ERVIN DRAKE, IRVIN GRAHAM,
JIMMY SHIRL, and AL STILLMAN

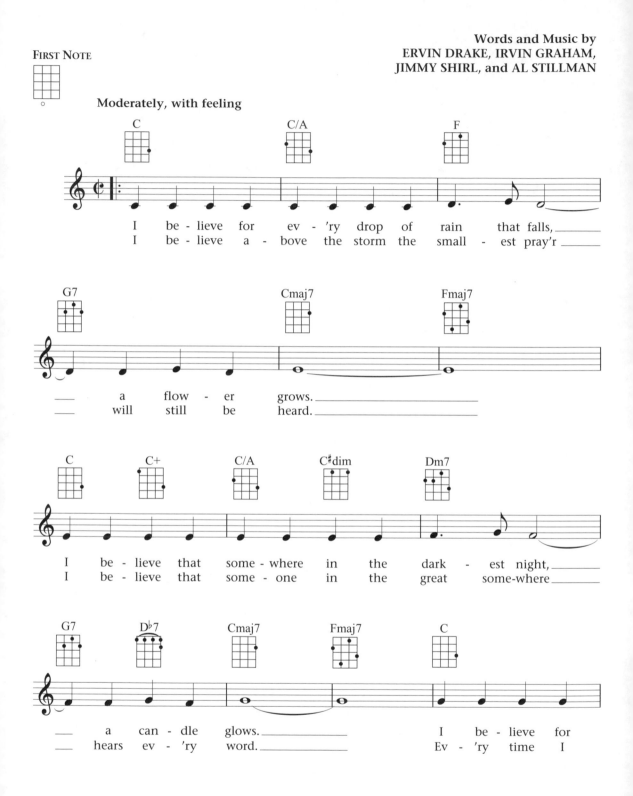

ev - 'ry - one who goes a - stray,_____ some - one will
hear a new - born ba - by cry,_____ or touch a

come_____ to show the way._____
leaf,_____ or see the

I be - lieve,_____ I be - lieve.

sky, _____ then I know why I be -

lieve!

Faith is believing what you know ain't so.

— *Mark Twain*

I Saw The Light

Words and Music by
HANK WILLIAMS

FIRST NOTE

Lively

1. I wan - dered so aim - less,
2. Just like a blind man I
3. I was a fool to

life filled with sin. I would - n't
wan - dered a - lone. Wor - ries and
wan - der and stray. Straight is the

let my dear Sav - ior in. _____
fears I claimed for my own. _____
gate and nar - row the way. _____

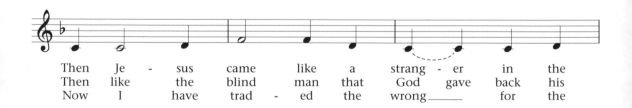

Then Je - sus came like a strang - er in the
Then like the blind man that God gave back his
Now I have trad - ed the wrong _____ for the

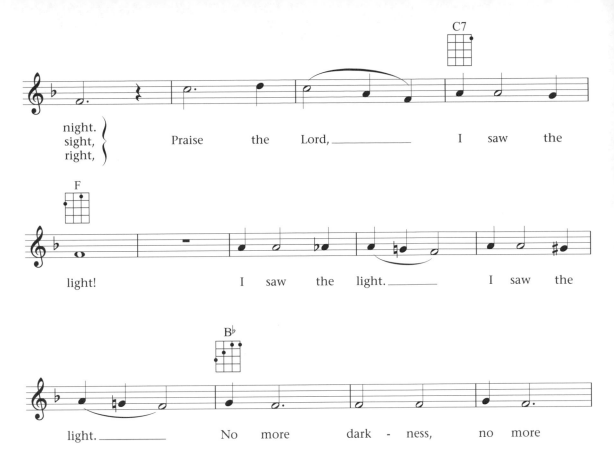

night.
sight, Praise   the   Lord, _____   I   saw   the
right,

light!   I   saw   the   light. _____   I   saw   the

light. _____   No   more   dark - ness,   no   more

night. _____   Now   I'm   so   hap - py,   no   sor - row   in

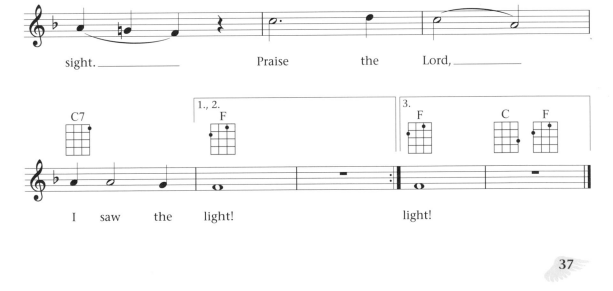

sight. _____   Praise   the   Lord, _____

I   saw   the   light!   light!

If I Had A Hammer

Words and Music by
LEE HAYS and PETE SEEGER

all _____ o - ver this land. _____

Additional Lyrics

2. If I had a bell, I'd ring it in the morning,
   I'd ring it in the evening, all over this land.
   I'd ring out danger, I'd ring out a warning,
   I'd ring out love between my brothers and my sisters,
   all over this land.

3. If I had a song, I'd sing it in the morning,
   I'd sing it in the evening, all over this land.
   I'd sing out danger, I'd sing out a warning,
   I'd sing out love between my brothers and my sisters,
   all over this land.

4. Well, I got a hammer, and I've got a bell,
   And I've got a song to sing, all over this land.
   It's the hammer of justice, it's the bell of freedom,
   it's the song about love between my brothers and my sisters,
   all over this land.

I don't like to hear cut-and-dried sermons. When I hear a man preach, I like to see him act as if he were fighting bees.

—*Abraham Lincoln*

In The Garden

Words and Music by
C. AUSTIN MILES

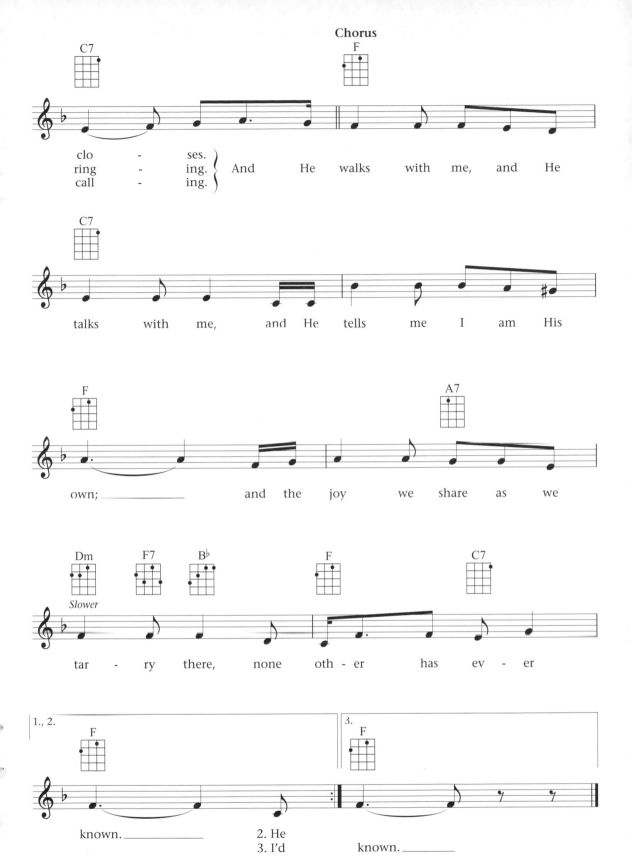

Chorus

clo - ses.
ring - ing.
call - ing.

And He walks with me, and He talks with me, and He tells me I am His own; _____ and the joy we share as we tar - ry there, none oth - er has ev - er

1., 2.
known. _____
2. He
3. I'd

3.
known. _____

In The Sweet By And By

Words by
SANFORD F. BENNETT

Music by
J. P. WEBSTER

| C | F | C | | | G | | G7 |

there.
rest.
days.

In the sweet by and by, we shall meet on that beau-ti-ful

| C | | C7 | | F |

shore; in the sweet by and by, we shall

| C | G7 | 1., 2. C F C | 3. C F C |

meet on that beau-ti-ful shore.

2. We shall
3. To our shore.

PRAISE HIM!

PRAISE HIM!

Sing with us at Sunday School next Sunday

Come!
We'll expect you!

"Come, let us sing unto the Lord." —Psalm 95:1

Joyful, Joyful, We Adore Thee

Words by
HENRY VAN DYKE

Music by
LUDWIG VAN BEETHOVEN

1. Joy - ful, joy - ful, we a - dore thee,
2. All thy works with joy sur - round thee,
3. Thou art giv - ing and for - giv - ing,

God of glo - ry, Lord of love; hearts un - fold like
earth and heaven re - flect thy rays, stars and an - gels
ev - er bless - ing, ev - er blest, well - spring of the

flowers be - fore thee, prais - ing thee, their sun a - bove.
sing a - round thee, cen - ter of un - bro - ken praise.
joy of liv - ing, o - cean - depth of hap - py rest!

Melt the clouds of sin and____ sad - ness; drive the____ dark of
Field and for - est, vale and____ moun - tain, bloom - ing____ mea - dow,
Thou our Fa - ther, Christ our____ Broth - er: all who____ live in

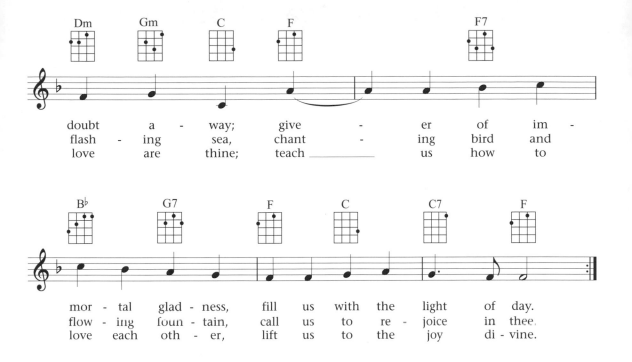

doubt a - way; give - er of im -
flash - ing sea, give chant - ing of bird and
love are thine; teach _____ us how to

mor - tal glad - ness, fill us with the light of day.
flow - ing foun - tain, call us to re - joice in thee.
love each oth - er, lift us to the joy di - vine.

Easter Sunrise Services, Hollywood Bowl, Hollywood, California

Just A Closer Walk With Thee

Traditional
Arranged by
KENNETH MORRIS

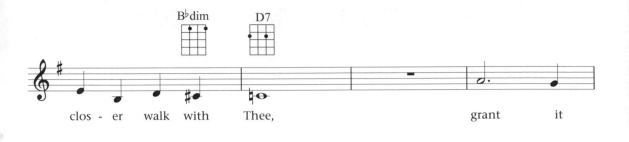

B♭dim   D7

clos - er walk with Thee,   grant it

G

Je - sus is my plea, _____   dai - ly

G7   C   C#dim   G

walk - ing close to Thee, _____   let it be, dear

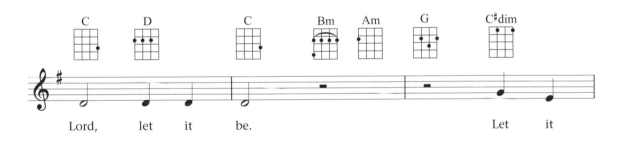

C   D   C   Bm   Am   G   C#dim

Lord, let it be.   Let it

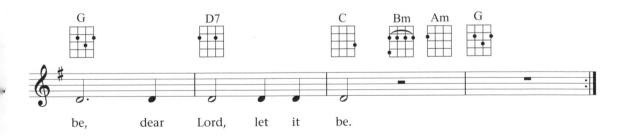

G   D7   C   Bm   Am   G

be, dear Lord, let it be.

Keep On The Sunny Side

Words and Music by
A. P. CARTER and GARY GARETT

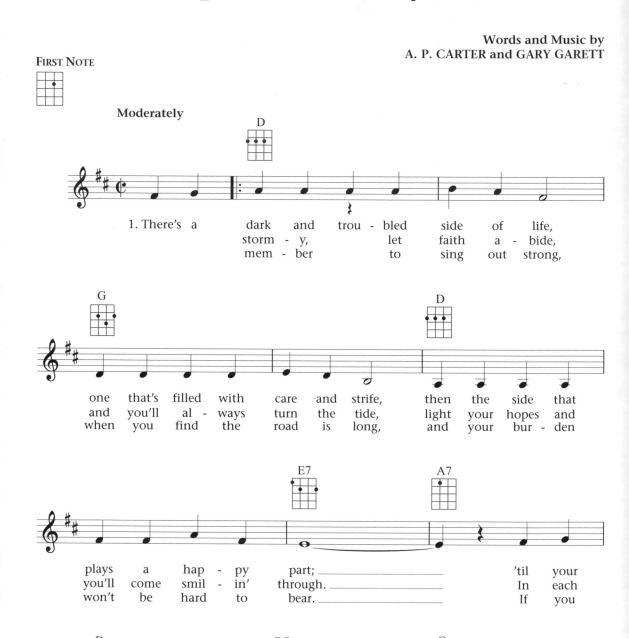

1. There's a   dark   and   trou - bled   side   of   life,
storm - y,   let   faith   a - bide,
mem - ber   to   sing   out   strong,

one   that's   filled   with   care   and   strife,   then   the   side   that
and   you'll   al - ways   turn   the   tide,   light   your   hopes   and
when   you   find   the   road   is   long,   and   your   bur - den

plays   a   hap - py   part;   'til   your
you'll   come   smil - in'   through.   In   each
won't   be   hard   to   bear.   If   you

span   of   life   is   done,   find   your   place   be - neath   the
life   there   must   be   rain,   but   you'll   ban - ish   ev - 'ry
learn   to   wear   a   smile,   you   will   short - en   ev - 'ry

sun, and the sun - shine will bright - en up your
pain, if you pic - ture will that rain - bow in the
trial, for the laugh - ter will drive a - way your

Chorus

heart. _____
blue. _____
care. _____

Keep on the sun - ny side,

al - ways on the sun - ny side, keep on the sun - ny side of

life. _____ It will help you ev - 'ry day, it will

bright - en all the way, if you keep on the sun - ny side of

life. _____

life. _____
2. When life's
3. Just re - life. _____

Let There Be Peace On Earth

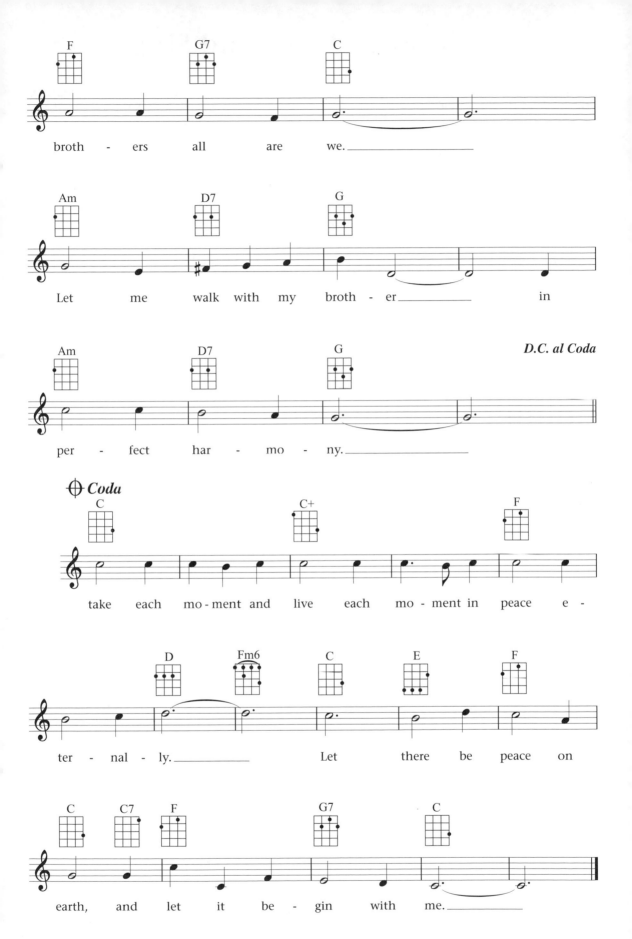

Lift Ev'ry Voice And Sing

Words by
JAMES WELDON JOHNSON

Music by
J. ROSAMOND JOHNSON

1. Lift ev-'ry voice and sing, 'til earth and heav-en ring, ring with the har-mo-nies of lib-er-ty. Let our re-joic-ing rise high as the list-'ning
2. Ston-y the road we trod, bit-ter the chast-'ning rod, fell in the days when hope un-born had died. Yet with a stead-y beat, have not our wear-ry
3. God of our wea-ry years, God of our si-lent tears, Thou who hast brought us thus far on the way. Thou who hast by Thy might, led us in-to the

May The Good Lord Bless And Keep You

Words and Music by
MEREDITH WILLSON

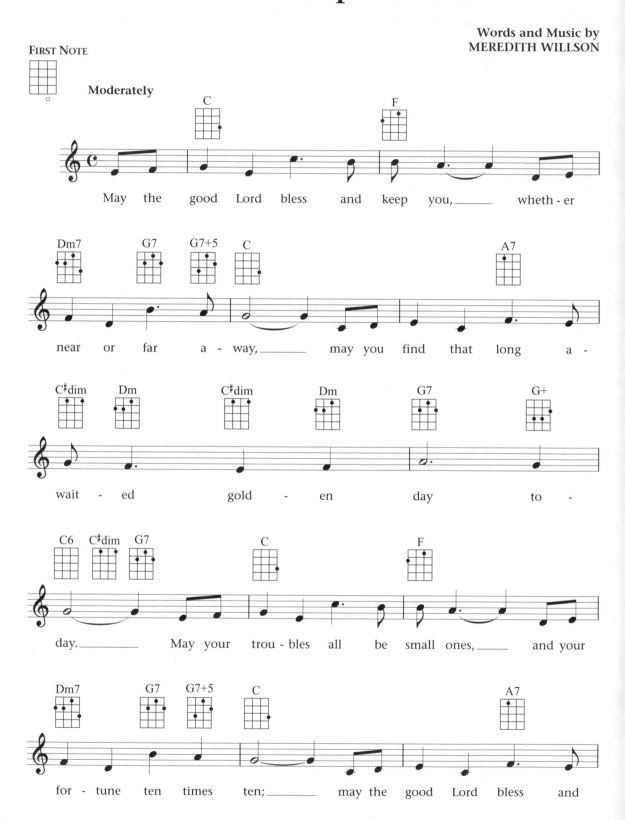

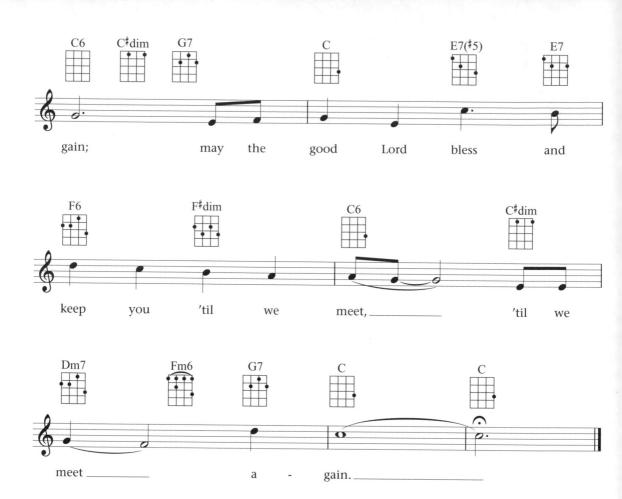

C6   C#dim   G7   C   E7(#5)   E7

gain;   may   the   good   Lord   bless   and

F6   F#dim   C6   C#dim

keep   you   'til   we   meet, _____   'til   we

Dm7   Fm6   G7   C   C

meet _____   a - gain. _____

Kum-Bah-Yah

Traditional

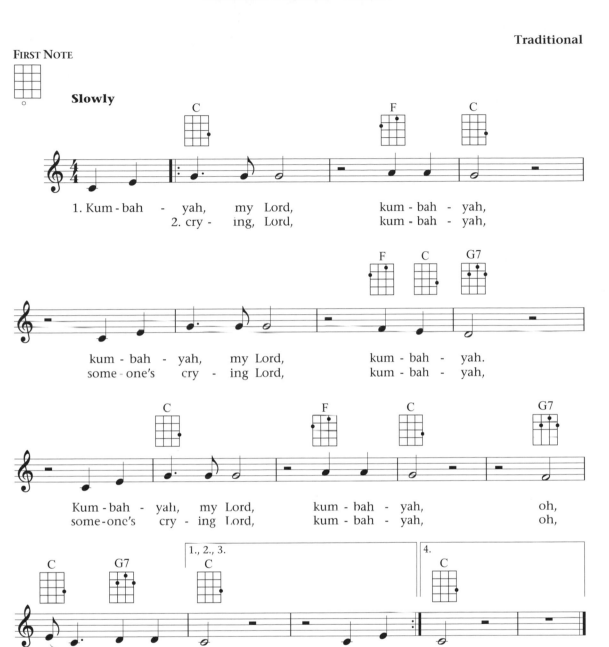

Additional Lyrics

3. Someone's singing, Lord, kum-bah-yah…
4. Someone's praying, Lord, kum-bah-yah…

Morning Has Broken

Words by
ELEANOR FARJEON

Traditional
Gaelic Melody

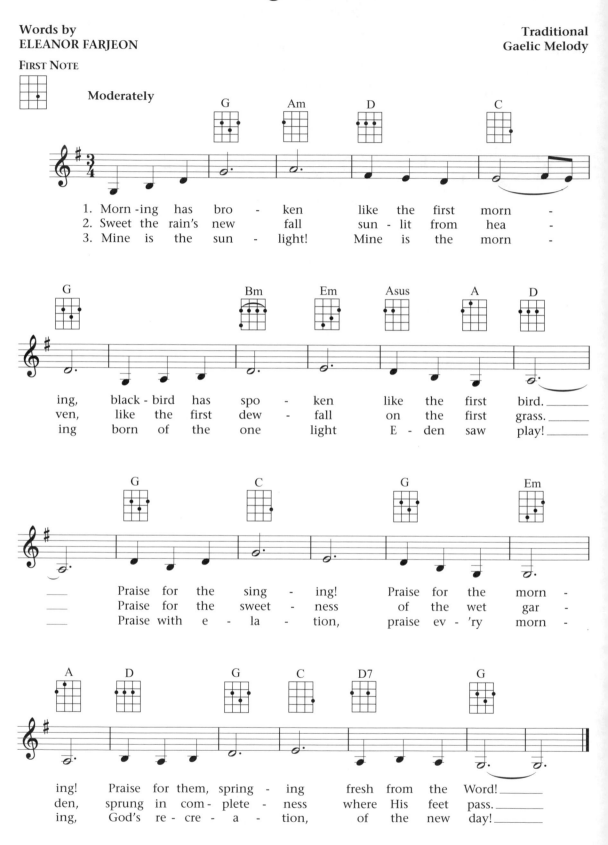

Nearer, My God, To Thee

Words by
SARAH FULLER ADAMS

Music by
LOWELL MASON

FIRST NOTE

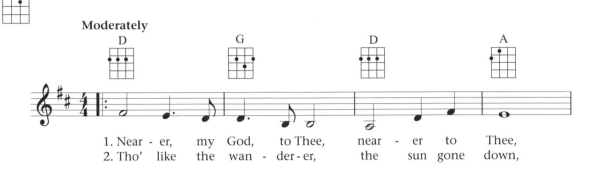

1. Near - er, my God, to Thee, near - er to Thee,
2. Tho' like the wan - der - er, the sun gone down,

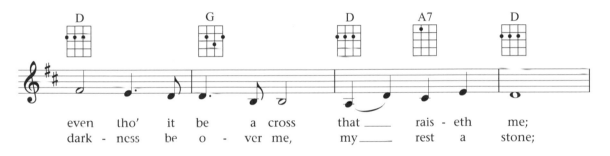

even tho' it be a cross that _____ rais - eth me;
dark - ness be o - ver me, my _____ rest a stone;

still all my song shall be) near - er, my God to Thee,
yet in my dreams I'd be)

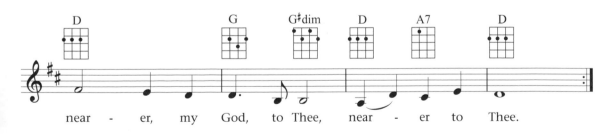

near - er, my God, to Thee, near - er to Thee.

Additional Lyrics

3. There let the way appear,
steps unto Heav'n,
all that Thou sendest me,
in mercy giv'n;
angels to beckon me…
nearer, my God, to Thee, *etc.*

4. Then with my waking thoughts,
bright with Thy praise,
out of my stony grief,
Bethel I'll raise;
so by my woes to be
nearer, my God, to Thee, *etc.*

One Earth, One Sky

Words by
ALISON HUBBARD

Music by
KIM OLER

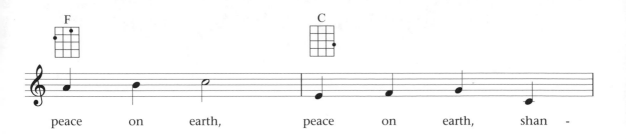

peace on earth, peace on earth, shan -

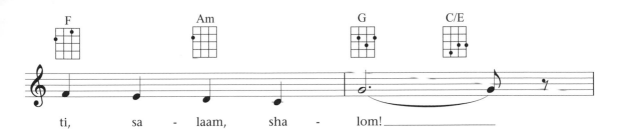

ti, sa - laam, sha - lom!_____

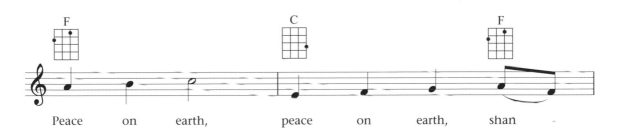

Peace on earth, peace on earth, shan -

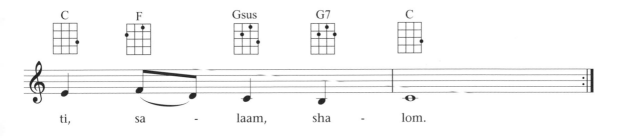

ti, sa - laam, sha - lom.

There never was a good war or a bad peace.

—Benjamin Franklin

Precious Lord, Take My Hand

Words and Music by
THOMAS A. DORSEY

When my way grows ___ drear, pre-cious Lord, lin - ger
When the dark - ness ap - pears and the night draws ___

near, ___ when my life ___ is ___ al - most ___
near, ___ and the day ___ is ___ past and ___

gone. ___ Hear my cry, hear my ___
gone, ___ at the riv - er I ___

call. ___ Hold __ my hand, lest I fall, ___ take __ my
stand, ___ guide __ my feet, hold my hand, ___

D.C.
(last time to Fine)

hand, ___ pre - cious Lord, ___ lead me home. ___

Swing Low, Sweet Chariot

Traditional

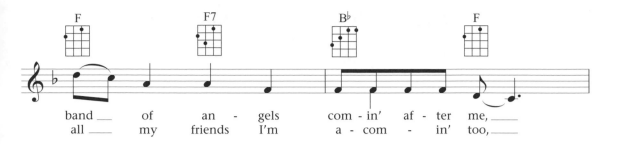

band ___ of an - gels com - in' af - ter me, ____
all ___ my friends I'm a - com - in' too, ____

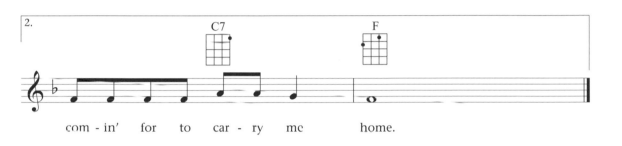

1.

com - in' for to car - ry me home. Swing

2.

com - in' for to car - ry me home.

Praise God From Whom
All Blessings Flow

Words by
THOMAS KEN

Traditional Melody

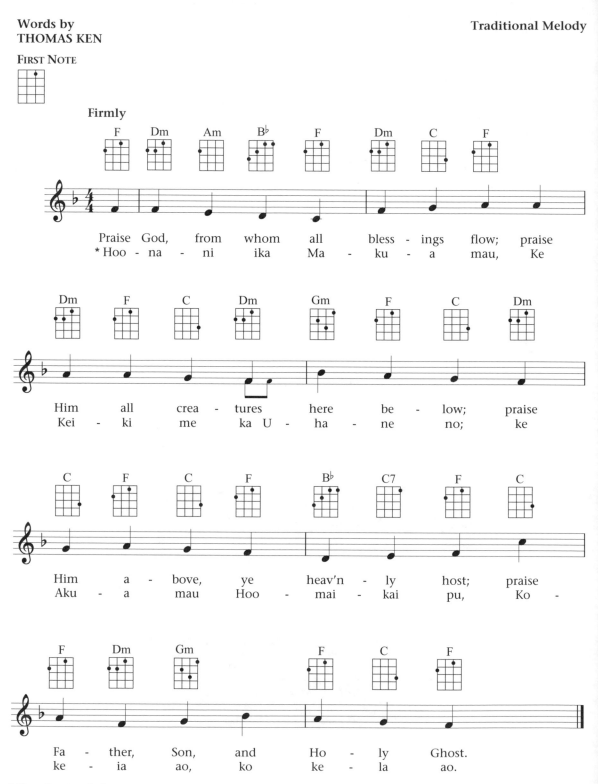

Hawaiian translation

This Little Light Of Mine

Traditional

We Shall Overcome

Musical and Lyrical Adaption by
ZILPHIA HORTON, FRANK HAMILTON,
GUY CARAWAN, and PETE SEEGER

Moderately slow, with determination

1. We shall o - ver - come, _____
2. We'll walk hand - in - hand, _____

we shall o - ver - come, _____ we shall o - ver -
we'll walk hand - in - hand, _____ we'll walk hand - in -

come some day. _____
hand some day. _____

Oh, _____ deep in my heart I do be -

lieve we shall o - ver - come some -

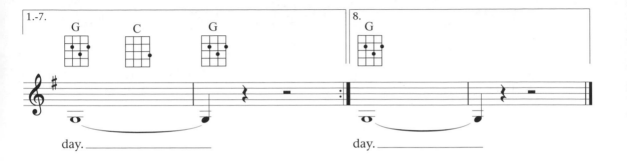

day. _____   day. _____

Additional Lyrics

3. We are not afraid, we are not afraid,
   we are not afraid today, *etc.*

4. We shall stand together, we shall stand together,
   we shall stand together, now, *etc.*

5. The truth will make us free, the truth will make us free,
   the truth will make us free someday, *etc.*

6. The Lord will see us through, the Lord will see through,
   the Lord will see us through someday, *etc.*

7. We shall be like Him, we shall be like Him,
   we shall be like Him someday, *etc.*

8. We shall live in peace, we shall live in peace,
   we shall live in peace someday, *etc.*

B lessed are the peacemakers:
for they shall be called the
children of God.

— Matthew 5:9

What A Friend We Have In Jesus

Words by
JOSEPH SCRIVEN

Music by
CHARLES C. CONVERSE

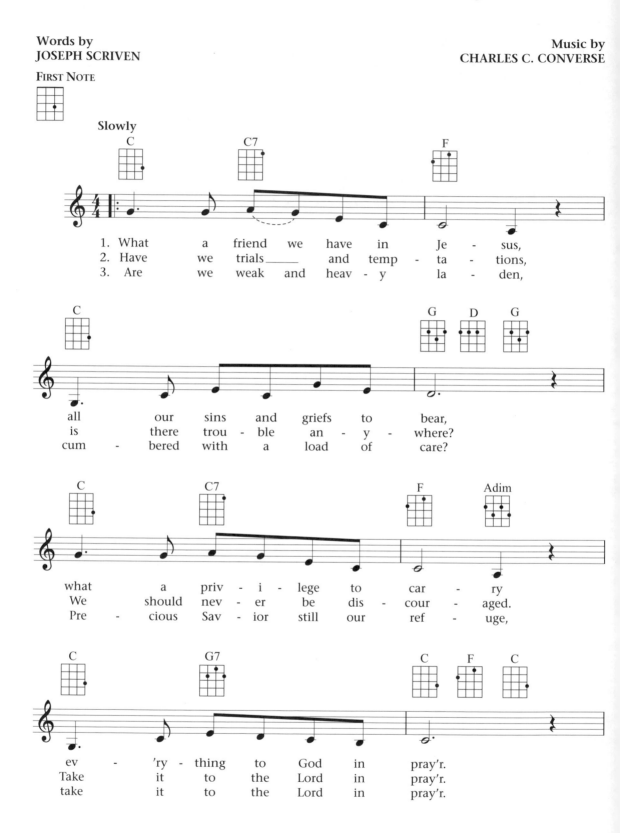

1. What a friend we have in Je - sus,
2. Have we trials_____ and temp - ta - tions,
3. Are we weak and heav - y la - den,

all our sins and griefs to bear,
is there trou - ble an - y - where?
cum - bered with a load of care?

what a priv - i - lege to car - ry
We should nev - er be dis - cour - aged.
Pre - cious Sav - ior still our ref - uge,

ev - 'ry - thing to God in pray'r.
Take it to the Lord in pray'r.
take it to the Lord in pray'r.

O what peace we of - ten for - feit,
Can we find a friend so faith - ful,
Do thy friends de - spise, for - sake thee?

o what need - less pain we bear,
who will all our sor - rows share?
Take it to the Lord in pray'r.

all be - cause we do not car - ry
Je - sus knows our ev - 'ry weak - ness,
In His arms He'll take and shield thee

1., 2.

ev - 'ry - thing to God in pray'r.
take it to the Lord in pray'r.

3.

3. thou wilt find a sol - ace there.

What A Wonderful World

Words and Music by
GEORGE DAVID WEISS
and BOB THIELE

FIRST NOTE

Moderately Slow

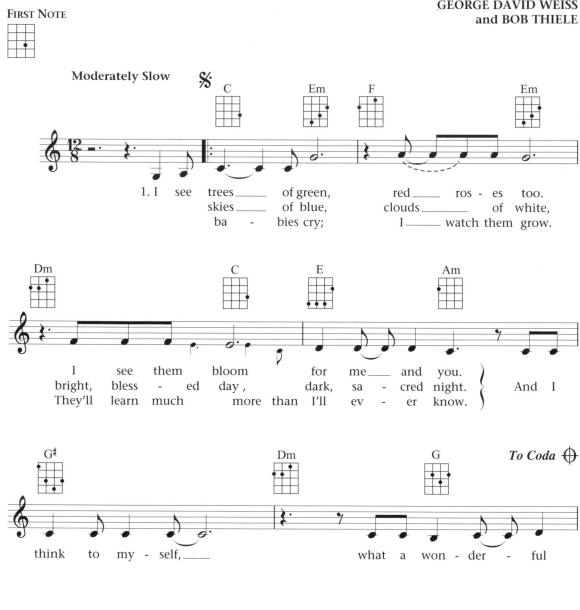

1. I see trees____ of green, red____ ros - es too.
   skies____ of blue, clouds_____ of white,
   ba - bies cry; I____ watch them grow.

I see them bloom for me____ and you.
bright, bless - ed day, dark, sa - cred night. And I
They'll learn much more than I'll ev - er know.

think to my - self,____ what a won - der - ful

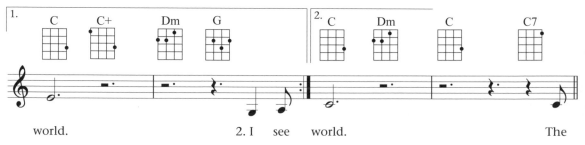

1.
world. 2. I see

2.
world. The

What The World Needs Now Is Love

Words by
HAL DAVID

Music by
BURT BACHARACH

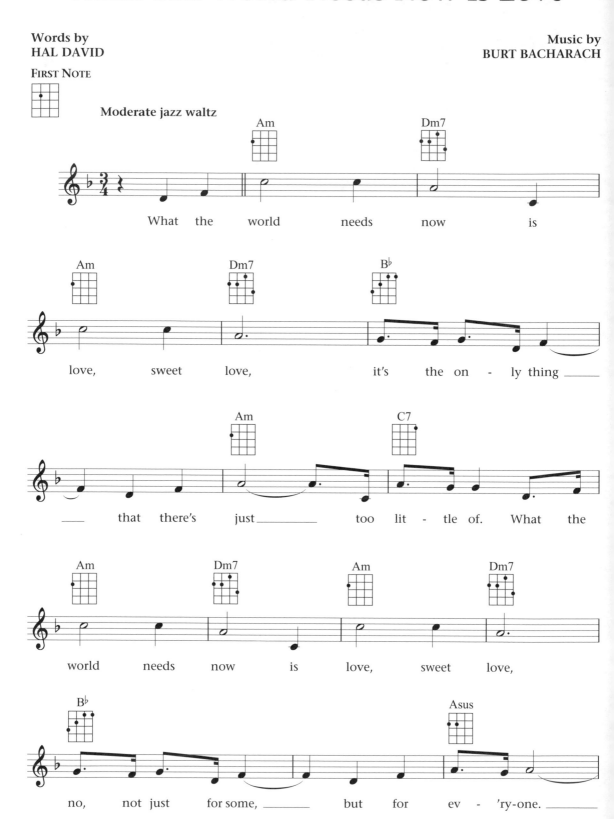

When The Saints Go Marching In

Traditional

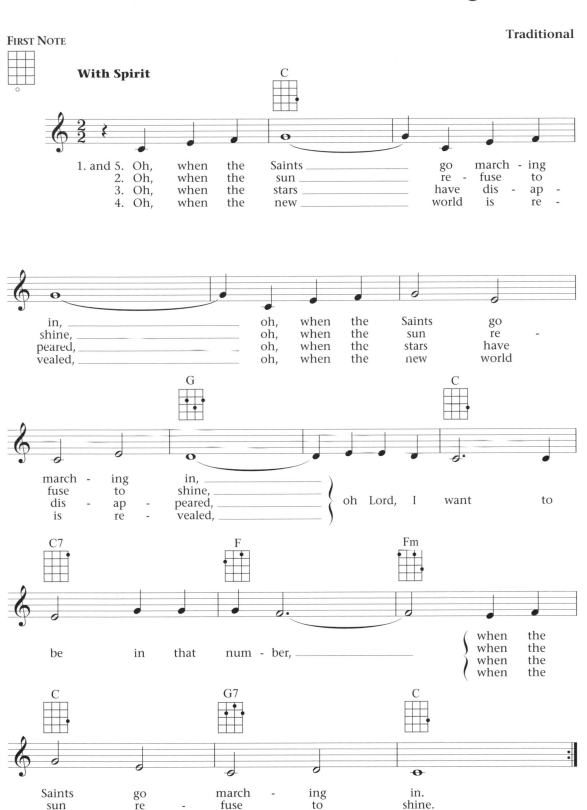

Will The Circle Be Unbroken

Traditional

wait - ing   in the   sky,   Lord,___ in the   sky.

Additional Lyrics

2. Lord I told the undertaker,
   "Undertaker, please drive slow,
   for this body you are hauling,
   Lord, I hate to see her go."
   Chorus

3. I followed close behind her,
   tried to hold up and be brave,
   but I could not hide my sorrow
   when they laid her in the grave.
   Chorus

4. Went back home, Lord. My home was lonesome,
   since my mother, she was gone.
   All my brothers, sisters, crying,
   What a home so sad and lone.
   Chorus

Let no one ever come to you

without leaving better and happier.

Be the living expression of God's kindness;

kindness in your face, kindness in your eyes,

kindness in your smile.

— *Mother Teresa*

Remember now thy Creator . . .

We missed you at Sunday School

Be sure to come next Sunday . . .

"Remember now thy Creator in the days of thy youth."
—*Ecclesiastes 12:1*